# THE 21ST CENTURY LAWRENCE OF ARABIA: FIGHTING INSURGENCY THROUGH GOOD GOVERNANCE

There is little dispute that the 21st Century begins with a U.S. military focused on counterinsurgency strategies designed around defeating global extremism. Conventional military threats no longer dominate the international diplomatic front or our military operational planning and doctrine focus. Instead, our U.S. civilian and military leadership face threats that demand a shift in how we see the enemy, ourselves, and organizationally train and equip for combat. Indeed, the very word combat in essence is a part of this transformation and redefinition. Non lethal objectives and tasks today are arguably more relevant, than the use of military fires and kinetic force applications. Civilian populations not enemy formations become the center of gravity for metrics in winning or losing in this Global War on Terrorism (GWOT). The question then remains, how do you 'win' the population as a means to defeat the insurgency? This paper argues that the answer lies in our military's ability to affectively partner and support host nation local governance.

The "unanticipated collapse of Iraq's infrastructure" following the March 2003 invasion left the U.S. led coalition with a daunting task of providing immediate national, sub-national, regional, and local governance support to the Iraqi people.[1] The immediate results were dismal and likely contributed to the widespread breakdown in rule of law, loss of essential services, and the nexus for the Iraqi insurgency. The Office for Reconstruction and Humanitarian Assistance (ORHA), stood up in February 2003 to assist the post invasion objectives, was "not designed or capable to cope with this void in governmental leadership" and competencies.[2] The Coalition Provisional Authority

(CPA) quickly replaced the ORHA in late May 03 but failed also to recognize the size and scope of the reconstruction requirements and governance problems that transcended all levels of Iraqi society. The resulting absence of an Iraqi or Department of State (DOS) sponsored authoritative decision making governing entity left U.S. military forces by default involved in or responsible for governance oversight. Nearly seven years later, the U.S. military still finds itself engaged and supporting local Iraqi governance, but not without some hard lessons. Counterinsurgency (COIN) lessons in general we can also conclude will drive current and future changes in all battlefield operating systems. Categories like command and control, precision munitions, and force structure to name a few rank as top concerns and issues for Department of Defense's (DOD) military strategist and scholars alike.

Notwithstanding, these topics as well as others will assist our military and civilian leadership in planning and adapting our military for future counterinsurgency warfare settings. Perhaps the most decisive lesson in COIN operations is our role, support, and involvement in local host nation governance. LTG David Barno, former commander of U.S. and coalition forces in Afghanistan, summed this issue up best when he reflected that "leadership… in an irregular warfare demands a broader set of skills than those required of conventional war at the same level. Where we fall short as leaders is understanding our requirements across the increasingly important non-military sphere and their centrality to success in irregular warfare."[3]

One can deduce that winning in a COIN environment must entail a significant military focus in non military tasks. The most complex non lethal task is arguably assisting local officials in establishing effective host nation civic services that support population stability and quality of life. In a recent Military Review counterinsurgency article, Department of State counterterrorism coordinator Dan Green highlighted this point by reminding all of us that "incorporating political goals" and good governance objectives in military planning are vital in winning the counterinsurgency fight.[4] From the strategic level down to the tactical level, our military's role in civic assistance must transcend the entire leadership hierarchy. Junior Non Commissioned Officers (NCOs) today unlike previous years, will likely "impact our nations foreign policy goals" through their personal engagements with local host nation officials.[5] Our charter as an military organization remains the ability to culturally institutionalize this COIN task as a necessary means to an end in conflict resolution. This paper will discuss and articulate recommendations in our current COIN training strategies, in theater partnership alignments, intelligence systems, and organizational adaptability in supporting local host nation governmental institutions. As a framework for discussion and logical proposals, this document focuses on current operations in Iraq and Afghanistan while looking to the past for similar parallel issues. Analyzing COIN with the governance line of operation as the main effort could very well provide the necessary solutions in winning in today's 21st Century counterinsurgency conflicts.

## Train as You Fight

> In the long run, developing better governance will probably affect the lives of the populace more than any other COIN activities. When well executed, these actions may eliminate the root causes of the insurgency.[6]

The above statement extracted straight from our counterinsurgency field manual reflects our Army's vision on the importance of governance in COIN operations. Assisting local governance as a means to an end in counterinsurgency warfare is sound guidance found throughout much of our recent updated doctrinal materials. FM 7-15, the Army's Universal Task list further complements our COIN manual with definitive instructions on military support to local civil authorities through " developing effective host nation governance at the local level before developing governance institutions and processes throughout the state."[7] Even our joint publications provide additional clarity on the role governance plays in counterinsurgency operations. JP3-0 states:

> Committed forces must sustain the legitimacy of the operation and of the host nation government.....Legitimacy also means the local populace's perception of their own internal government. Civil military operations that support local governments allows for the populace to perceive that the government has genuine authority to govern and use proper agencies for support.[8]

The difficult challenge is our Army and perhaps DOD in general fail to adequately train conventional forces on civic responsibilities relating to host nation governance. The preponderance of tasks associated with preparing for today's COIN operations focus primarily on force protection and kinetic skill sets. Indeed, the latest FORCES COMMAND (FORSCOM) Army OIF/OEF tasks dated 17Nov09 mandates over 70 major tasks encompassing individual through collective training requirements for deploying units.[9] All COIN and conventional tasks prescribed within the message cover a wide range of lethal and non lethal training prerequisites; yet, fall short in addressing host nation governance tasks. Ironically once units deploy, most discover their attention focused on assisting, supporting, and in some cases leading local governments or host nation security forces. A recent RAND article that looked at COIN in the Muslim world estimated that nearly 40,000 US Soldiers and Marines were currently performing "civic functions" in support of reconstruction and good governance.[10] This number, while certainly not indicative of the entire force, does represent a sizable military population that is dedicated to supporting or advising host nation governance. Retired Army officer

LTC John Nagl, who has written extensively on counterinsurgency warfare, also stated that when looking at the Afghanistan surge "a renewed U.S. commitment to funding grass roots development and governance must accompany the influx of troops."[11]

The apparent observation then becomes changing our military training culture from a bullet centric mentality to that involving mayoral responsibilities. This is not to say that we should forgo kinetic or lethal training and validation. Quite the contrary, the complexity of our weapon systems and the risks associated with fighting a radicalized enemy demand a pre-deployment effort centered on fighting. This kinetic training methodology, however, is only half the battle – the defensive side. Winning a counterinsurgency campaign requires thinking offensively in our training by looking as our field manual directs, at the "root cause of insurgencies."[12] Failing to see the enemy through this lens may "often slow or prevent the timely resolution of the conflict" as seen in both Iraq and Afghanistan today.[13]

Developing or changing an ineffective local government gets at this root cause in many counterinsurgency campaigns. The difficulty for many military leaders is the required mental energy, civic appreciation, and overcoming military bias towards political solutions. If left unchecked though, corrupt or weak host nation governing bodies may often fuel an insurgency rather than suppress it. In a recent interview, General Stanley McChrystal, Commander Multi-National Forces Afghanistan, articulated that "most of the people fighting the U.S. in Afghanistan were motivated by local and personal grievances. They want more of a voice in governance or they want jobs."[14] Nagl complemented this point by further highlighting that "until the United States and ISAF get their approach to 'local communities' right, those communities will not

5

decisively turn against the insurgency.[15] What the military can get right is seeing this problem well before we enter the battlefield.

Investing in home station training resources that educate and replicate host nation governance situations is a start in the right direction. The obvious counter argument to governance related training is this is not our job. Unfortunately, DOS and other civilian agencies are drastically under resourced to meet this manpower intensive responsibility. This fact will likely not change in the near future or the years ahead. The question then becomes if not them, then who? The answer as we have already observed rests upon our military leaders and forward deployed units.

A well founded second concern lies in our already full pre-deployment training plate. Most unit commanders already acknowledge the task list associated with their home station training calendar leaves little room for new requirements. Adding additional non-lethal training related material in a condensed seven to nine month train up period, will likely do more to degrade a unit's overall preparation than to assist it.

The likely solution equals a thorough review of our current training requirements against operational realities. Acknowledging the observation that leaders spend enormous time in theater time executing civic related functions, should cue our focus on ensuring we are training for the right tasks - not just the tasks common to military forces. Another viable option may be embedding English speaking former host nation civic leaders with U.S. Brigade Combat Teams (BCTs) well before the unit deploys. Similar to the Korean Augmentation to the United States Army (KATUSA) concept, company and higher leadership learn through day to day mentorship process as opposed to a formal training strategy. This concept while notably expensive and possess security vetting issues, might nonetheless offer the best in roads in transforming military leaders into an institution with a broader counterinsurgency mindset.

Other less formalized and ad hoc solutions are already making their way from the field back to units preparing for deployment. The key phrase though is "from the field" and not originating from our training base. Most deployed forces for example, recognizing the strategic support to governance importance develop local "anthropologist's guides" for the inbound replacing unit's train up and educational benefits.[16] These phamplets, booklets, and/or in some cases wiring diagrams assist all levels of leadership in gaining a better civic perspective in counterinsurgency warfare. Additionally, in 2007 while late in the learning process, the Center for Army Lessons Learned (CALL) did publish an extensive tool on understanding Iraqi governance. The document called the *Republic of Iraq District Government Field Manual* provided a comprehensive overview on Iraqi governmental institutions. The handbook's original intent was for training OIF State Department embedded Provisional Reconstruction Teams (ePRTs); however, due to a lack of related material for military forces this document possibly remains the best resource today for OIF deploying units.[17] The lessons offered in this overarching governance review suggested the complexity in understanding Iraqi governing procedures coupled with the historical and cultural dimensions. Several CALL Iraqi governance observations highlighted below demonstrate the difficulties military leaders may face if not fully versed in host nation civic awareness:

- Iraqi support to essential services does not by US standards have a clear chain of command on responsibility. The Amanat (mayor of Baghdad) for

7

example provides sewage, water, and trash services through the Beladiya (local municipalities); however, the Minister of Water also provides this same service in certain parts of Iraq and Baghdad for that matter.

- Electricity considered a municipality issue by western standards, is actually controlled by the Minister of Electricity.

- Governors of provinces and the governor of Baghdad have their own separate line of authority and responsibilities that often conflict with local districts and the Council of Representatives (COR).

- CPA Order 71 established the formal framework for sub-national Iraqi governance. The Minister of Finance (MOF) and Ministry of Planning and Cooperative Development (MOPCD) however resist supporting this order due to its western origin. As a result, local district councils struggle for financing and reconstruction aid.[18]

The challenge though is that governance information while in some cases available is just that, information. What is missing is a top driven training validation process that incorporates operational governance feedback lessons throughout our training systems.

Possibly the right step in redesigning our training methodology begins with defining governance from a service delivery standpoint. Here again operational lessons and doctrinal information are available but not universally acted upon. Field Manual 7-15 for example, provides overarching guidelines with prescriptive definitions on support to host nation governance. Effective local governance in the early stages of a counterinsurgency campaign as described in the FM "almost depends entirely on the ability to provide essential services to the people."[19]

This declaration speaks volumes for what leaders face in today's COIN environment. For illustration, during the first years of OIF U.S. military forces lacking support from other DOS and U.S. governmental agencies found themselves in direct oversight of these civic functions.[20] Planning and executing these tasks, however, were pursued "inconsistently and often incoherently by coalition military forces on the ground.[21] U.S. forces in Northern Iraq for example, ran Kirkuk with little input from Baghdad.[22] Other U.S. commanders and leaders lacking any formal knowledge base on Iraqi essential service support began relying heavily on informal actors. These wide range of actors notably tribal, religious, and militia leaders asserted their "practical autonomy" from the post Sadam Iraqi government - sometimes at the expense of good governance. In some Iraqi provinces military leadership gravitated towards tribal Shykhs as their "central point of contact often in direct competition with the newly formed Iraqi political parties."[23] Sheiks in Iraq and tribal elders in Afghanistan emerged in much of the rural areas as defacto governing bodies - even though not officially recognized by the central government.

While these informal governing bodies certainly played a critical role in reconciliation and security enhancements, they nonetheless frequently confused U.S. military leaders on their alleged official service related responsibilities. U.S commanders even though well intentioned, "failed to appreciate from the outset" complexities in tribal governance versus the state elected civic leaders."[24] Compounding the problem for U.S. Commanders both in Iraq and Afghanistan centered on governmental nuances that drove specific service support functions from the national to local level. In Iraq, preexisting laws (pre- Sadam) and the new Iraqi Republic 2005 Constitution - both complementing and conflicting with one another – dictated law and order and essential service delivery.  CALL described this in a recent report by stating: "the history of Iraq and Baghdad governance is quite complicated, owed to disparate sources: the constitution, pre-constitutional legislation, and custom."[25]  Each ministry for example has its own very distinctive approach to delivering services.  No uniformity in their approach as CALL noted in providing support to the local governorates. Complicating the issue was the CPA constitutional influence with western democratic values that many Iraqis felt were unconstitutional due to their origin.[26] Budget development and distribution was also problematic and difficult to trace.  Bottom up resource generation while supported under the constitution was not formally recognized by most of the Iraqi central government.  Money disbursement and priorities still remains largely the responsibility of the Iraqi federal government with little regional or district involvement.[27]

Similarly, Afghanistan governmental framework comes with its own set of complex challenges. Localized federations or provincial control dominate the Afghanistan political landscape.   Thomas Friedman from the New York Times stated as such when he observed that the "local" not central government "was the critical bridge" in our military's counterinsurgency goals.[28] John Nagl's recent analysis on Afghanistan also reflected that the "concept of official governance should be expanded by incorporating traditional structures such as the village and district shuras."[29] Both comments while originating from a western stance indicate a potentially painful lesson in that governing in Afghanistan is not the same as Iraq or anyplace else in the world.

One can infer that inserting coalition military leaders into the host nation governmental process with minimal instruction or training can potentially do more damage and fuel societal frustration even though well intentioned. If we expect an end state that the state or country can perform such functions as "law and order, economic management, public health, and education," then it is imperative that military leaders are familiar with their supporting roles in achieving this objective.[30] The only solution is a greater emphasis on governance support during home station preparation as opposed to in theater trial and error.

Corollary to military assistance to governance entails a thorough understanding in resource and budgetary responsibilities. Again our doctrine and historical evidence lead the way in reminding U.S. military leaders on their roles resourcing local governance. FM 3-24 states that "special funds accomplishing beneficial tasks can begin the process of establishing host nation government legitimacy. Some of these sample tasks include: trash pickup, road improvements, water purification, and distributing supplies."[31] Additionally, LTC David Galula, a 20th Century French expert on counterinsurgency warfare described 'funds' as a critical element in supporting local governments "with the minimal amount of red tape."[32] While our doctrine and history acknowledge the funding importance to local governance, our military as an institution struggles with preparing leaders adequately for this inherently counterinsurgency task.

As we view this issue from an operational lens, both Iraq and Afghanistan currently have robust public service agendas designed to reconstruct years of neglect and stimulate local economies. The monetary costs associated with this public sector service aid are enormous and far surpass most U.S. military leader's previous

11

experience and training base. Typically in both theaters, U.S. forces not only manage and distribute large sums of money but additionally assist in prioritization and budgetary focus for the local governing officials. Commanders and leaders at all levels, find themselves planning, supporting, and in some cases executing local host nation financial aid with previously little training or awareness. The Commander's Emergency Response Program (CERP), a case in point, was "established to focus on local small-scale projects and enable brigade and division commanders to spend up to $50,000 and $100,000 respectively for reconstruction projects."[33] CERP, while notably very successful in the later stages of OIF and OEF was more from in theater experiences than from any home station training focus. Other reconstruction aid such as the Congressionally allocated Iraqi Relief and Reconstruction Fund (IRRF) provided significant monetary support towards civic revitalization; however, it also failed in the OIF early stages due in large part to confusion on CPA versus military planning and oversight responsibilities.[34] U.S. commanders on the ground often did not know the: who, what, and the why on when reconstruction aid mysteriously arrived in their sector. They certainly had the "pulse of the people" on the ground but were challenged in connecting requirements at street level with resources available at the national level.[35]

Today, through the help of the U.S. military, significant financial aid is reaching a broad range of Iraqi and Afghan government and civic agencies; yet, not without years of discovery learning – largely at the expense of the Iraqi/Afghanistan population and the U.S. taxpayer. Suffice to say, commanding or leading in counterinsurgency warfare requires skills that advance well beyond just fighting. Regardless of the 'how' we conduct governance training, our current strategy must align or mirror with the majority of the operational tasks being performed in a COIN environment. Wall Street journalist Michael Phillips noted this point on a recent embed with an army cavalry squadron in Afghanistan by stating that most leaders were as much "sociologist as Soldiers."[36] He further observed that most commanders required "the sensitivity of a social worker, the cultural awareness of an anthropologist and the deal-making abilities a big-city mayor."[37] Balancing our future COIN training strategies with increased emphasis on governance and civic awareness is perhaps the best tool in conflict resolution. Understanding the campaign end state from this context may very well promote a train as you fight shift in tasks focusing more on civil support than a lethal fire and maneuver methodology.

Engagement through Partnership

> You [military professionals] must know something about strategy and tactics and....logistics, but also economics and politics and diplomacy and history....You must understand that few of the important problems of our time have been finally solved by military power.[38]

Since the end of the Cold War, the United States DOS civilian diplomatic corps has shrunk, not grown. Budget cuts, reduced staffing, and increased responsibilities worldwide have undermined DOS's diplomacy and assistance abroad.[39] The military has filled large gaps in our 21st Century global engagement strategy not to mention our civic responsibilities within Iraq and Afghanistan. Today, more than any time in our history, military leaders of all ranks find themselves in the unavoidable position in shaping foreign policy. A vivid illustration of this issue can be seen in Afghanistan where in early 2009 there were only 300 DOS personnel assigned to the theater compared to nearly 70,000 DOD personnel.[40]

Given these realities in U.S. foreign service shortages, the military increasingly is seen playing a major role in host nation government partnership. This civilian diplomatic deficiency requires military commanders to become, by default, the political advisors to the local, regional, or national host nation governing officials. As one young Marine lieutenant so aptly stated in Iraq when supporting local leaders in water distribution that, "this is something the State Department is suppose to handle but I was the Marine platoon commander on the ground, and I had to decide how and where the water would get distributed."[41]

Partnering with U.S. or foreign civic leaders, while perhaps not natural in our military culture is, nonetheless likely the most decisive mechanism in defeating an insurgency.  Galula articulated this point in terms of "living with the population" and viewing "politics as the active instrument of power in isolating the insurgent from the population." [42] He further added that "victory in counterinsurgency warfare is the permanent isolation of the insurgent from the population, isolation not enforced upon the population but maintained by and with the population."[43]  These words while nearly 50 years old still ring true for U.S. military leaders today.  Isolating the insurgent through effective politics (governance) or in other words local partnership, offers greater opportunities for tactical and strategic victory than anything else available in our COIN doctrine.  Insurgencies as a recent RAND article described "nearly always fail against governments that are representative, competent, and honest in the eyes of their citizens."[44]

The question then becomes the 'how' in partnership.  Most military commanders today have embedded Provincial Reconstruction Teams (ePRTs) or PRTs that assist and in some cases take the lead in partnering with local city or village councils.  ePRTs and PRTs play a valuable role in building local governments into effective governing bodies. Their part while somewhat new to the counterinsurgency environment does provide tactical and operational commanders a civic outreach capability that prior to 2006 did not exist.[45] Notwithstanding, ePRTs or PRTs relevancy in many areas of Iraq and Afghanistan still retain a significant core structure made up of military officers and Non Commissioned Officers. This fact coupled with a shortage in DOS foreign area service expertise dictate that military leaders remain engaged in the political, economic, and host nation governance COIN influence sphere. Subsequently, unity of effort between military leaders and their civilian counterparts may very well define the 'how' in governance solutions.

Unity of effort however, is easier said than done. U.S. civil-military working relationships in armed conflict have a history of friction and cultural mistrust. This disparity is certainly evident in both counterinsurgency campaigns today. Culturally our military tends to view conflict scenarios that reward success from a "fighting" standpoint and not "war winning" point of view.[46] DOS and other civilian inter-agencies often have the big "war winning" picture responsibility for COIN but lack capacity, manpower, and resources to affect change. LTG Barno, described this issue in a recent essay in which we fail as a military to see the "big picture" and don't understand the "vital importance of integrating the civil-military effort."[47] The reality he goes on to state is that "the civil resources be it manpower" or equipment will demand that military leaders and their organizations play a significant role in the "80% non-military dimension" of counterinsurgency warfare.[48] Unfortunately as LTG Barno articulates we [the military] tend to "go it alone" and not fully "harmonize" our efforts with civilian agencies focused on the same end state.[49] "Communicating and building relationships" with U.S. civilian

15

and host nation political constituents was just as important, he concludes if not more so than any tactical victory against the Taliban.  If the "embassy" failed in their mission as LTG Barno reminded his staff, then "we all fail in Afghanistan".[50] This senior leader COIN analysis provides invaluable partnership insights not only specific to Afghanistan but arguably relevant for any counterinsurgency setting.

Intelligence Support to Governance

Developing host nation civic relationships also demands that we rethink our intelligence strategies.  Seeing the enemy from a non-lethal lens is justifiably just as important in a counterinsurgency conflict, than our traditional conventional intelligence gathering view point. Our counterinsurgency doctrine reminds us that intelligence preparation in a COIN environment must analyze "civilian power and authority, society, culture, language, and social structures."[51] David Galula further reiterates this message by recommending a thorough analysis on the legitimacy of local leaders.[52] Unit commanders he suggests must "test" local leaders to determine their honesty and integrity in regards to good governance.  If deemed unworthy, these leaders must be removed.[53]

The paradigm shift for most leaders today is applying our intelligence gathering capacity in this venue.  Unfortunately, our military remains focused on the lethal targeting side as opposed to the full counterinsurgency spectrum.  MG Michael Flynn, Deputy CoS for Intelligence for the International Security Assistance Force in Afghanistan, recommends sweeping changes to our collection efforts based on this very same observation.  His recent well spoken article surmises that:

> The United States has focused the overwhelming majority of intelligence gathering and analytical brainpower on insurgent groups, yet our intelligence apparatus still finds itself unable to answer fundamental

16

questions about the environment in which we operate and the people we are trying to protect and persuade.[54]

Analyzing host nation governmental institutions from an intelligence stand point may therefore provide military planners and leaders significant insight on the countries civic infrastructure, capabilities, and governance interoperability's. Similar to conventional analysis on unit formations, commanders viewing governance from this vantage point have a far greater advantage and likely will respond with the desired friendly affects. MG Flynn strongly recommends this concept through re-tasking our analytical community along "geographical lines" and focused more on "district assessments covering governance, development and security."[55] Simply put, we must apply intelligence with less emphasis on our analytical technical systems and more towards the human element in counterinsurgency conflicts.

This is not to say that several military formations are not already applying this methodology on how they view or attack the enemy. Certainly at the battalion level, most units recognize the use of intelligence in a much broader role. In Afghanistan for example, battalion or squadron intelligence shops more and more are demonstrating competencies that are balanced towards civic issues than lethal targeting. This "encyclopedia of knowledge," as one squadron's leadership proposed, helps prevent the U.S. "from taking sides" against local entities.[56] Long standing internal grievances for instance if not understood upfront, could drive one faction or "aggrieved party" to embrace the Taliban or Al Qaeda more than any ideological beliefs.[57]

Applying our intelligence systems and structures across a much broader sphere requires more than just a focus at the battalion level. Brigade and higher intelligence capabilities also must remain relevant through a greater emphasis on seeing the enemy

17

through this lens. Regional, sub-national, and national governing systems by default are typically complicated and require paradigm changes on how we view collection in this area. Incorporating civil affairs teams, PRTs, and even putting analysts in the field as MG Flynn suggests gets at the collection requirements in seeing the enemy from this perspective. Nearly a decade later however, our military hierarchy still remains fixated on kinetic solutions as opposed to using intelligence to identify societal issues that fuel the insurgency. Perhaps the solution lies in our ability to adapt as an organization in order to maximize finite manning and equipping platforms in support of non-traditional civic or society targets.

## Organizational Adaptability to Support Host Nation Governance

> Essential elements of successful operations in Iraq included a keen understanding of the situation, integration of all arms and joint capabilities, the development and integration of indigenous forces, and military support to governance.[58]

The 2006 Israeli experience in Lebanon demonstrated bleak lessons in an Army that became over reliant on nation building at the expense of its core war fighting tasks. United States Military professor and scholar on U.S. Army Small Wars Gian Gentile suggests this is a "warning to all U.S. military planners against having an Army that has become so focused on COIN or irregular warfare that it can no longer fight battles against an enemy who has trained and organized to fight."[59] War as he argued is about fighting and suggests our Army must organize around this principle.[60] While one cannot argue this ominous point, the reality is to win in a counterinsurgency fight, you must look beyond the RPG and more towards the population. This is not to say we should allow ourselves to fall victim to a 2006 Lebanon like surprise; rather, adapting our organization against the environmental conflict realities is arguably the best answer in winning on any battlefield.

As we study this premises from a counterinsurgency view, organizational adaptability becomes perhaps more crucial than any high end conflict we may face. In particular how we organize to support civil or governance tasks may very well determine success or failure in a COIN environment. In this context, intelligence collection and analysis as previously discussed must now not only look at lethal targeting but also population discontent issues. Reengineering our intelligence systems to support a more holistic view as MG Flynn reminds us is founded on adaptability and flexibility within our formations. Colonel Christopher D. Kolenda a former squadron commander in Afghanistan, as a case in point, re-tasked his "intelligence shop to towards understanding the social relationships, economic disputes, and religious and tribal leaderships of the local communities."[61] This effort coupled with other adaptive strategies, profoundly reduced the number of lethal engagements between the insurgency. Villagers and tribal leaders began to see the U.S. and Afghanistan security forces as the ally as opposed to the Taliban or Al Qaeda operatives. This tactical battlefield example illustrates the criticality in one unit's adaptation towards population support. Interestingly at the strategic level one may view Vietnam as a potential case study on a military's organizational governance adaptation.

In Vietnam, prior to 1967 both Army and Marine units were conventionally focused on defeating the North Vietnamese Army (NVA) and Viet Cong guerrillas through search and destroy type operations. While tactically successful, operationally and strategically the war's outcome was very much in doubt. In late 1967, the Marines began incorporating pacification tactics in small unit operations. Pacification defined by the Marine Corps "was the military, political, economic, and social process of establishing or reestablishing local government responsive to and involving the participation of the people."[62] General C. Creighton Abrams Commander, U.S. Forces in Vietnam, recognized the validity in pacification as a means to the end and instituted the Civil Operations and Rural Development Support (CORDS) programs throughout South Vietnam. Both Army and Marines units were reorganized and in essence re-missioned to focus on "every level of the Vietnamese society."[63] Establishing local officials, supporting economic, public, and health improvements along with security to the population became the primary objective for most units throughout Vietnam. [64] Pacification, once it was "integrated under CORDS was generally led, planned, and executed well".[65] Unfortunately too late in the war to change the strategic outcome, CORDs and pacification nonetheless did demonstrate unit and military adaptability in supporting governance at the lowest level. Applicable to Iraq and Afghanistan today this suggested technique could very well assist military leaders at all levels in redefining their partnership responsibilities at all levels of governance.

Applying lessons from the past as well as recent COIN deployments, military organizations today are demonstrating positive governance adaptation trends. BCTs deploying to Iraq in 2010 for example are organized, manned, and equipped as Advise and Assist Brigades (AABs). This concept while still centrally focused on security assistance does take into account governmental support as a necessary means to end in counterinsurgency warfare. U.S. involvement in future counterinsurgencies conflicts must consider this principle particularly as it applies towards supporting local host nation civic authorities.

Conclusion

Victory in counterinsurgency warfare does not require that our military create "the development of a "modern European" or Middle Eastern state.[66] Success can be judged in a security environment that provides national stability, sovereignty, and good governance that meets "the basic needs of the people in terms of justice, economic opportunity, and political enfranchisement."[67] The latter as this paper proposes is arguably the most difficult and most complex for our U.S. military: difficult, though not impossible. Revamping our training strategy is obviously the first step in preparing leaders and units alike for this complex COIN condition. Understanding also partnership relationships with both U.S. civilian agencies and foreign governments from an execution standpoint is perhaps just as important in implementing any governance supporting strategies. Additionally, viewing civic and societal issues from an intelligence lens is vital in determining root cause insurgency issues that often are more non lethal than they are lethal. Finally and likely most importantly, we must institutionalize organizational adaptability focusing on governance as the primary defeat mechanism in counterinsurgency campaign. Fundamentally, our military must recognize that the means to the end in fighting the insurgency is not about the biggest weapon but rather how effective host nation governance is in supporting their own people. As the late T.E. Lawrence stated nearly 100 years ago "Irregular war is far more intellectual than a bayonet charge" remains an axiom of truth for all military leaders today.[68] Adaptability, social, and cultural awareness marked his success both on and off the battlefield a century ago. The quandary remains for 21st Century

21

counterinsurgency warfare leaders is our ability to also adapt and attack the enemy much differently than in previous decades.  Becoming the 21st Century Lawrence of Arabia is perhaps the goal in finding victory through good governance as opposed to winning battlefield engagements that may provide no long term solution.

<u>Endnotes</u>

[1] Eric Herring and Glen Rangwala, *Iraq in Fragments: The Occupation and Its Legacy* (Ithaca, New York: Cornell University Press,2006), 14.

[2] Ibid.

[3] LTG David Barno, "Command in Afghanistan 2003-2005: Three Key Lessons Learned" in *Commanding Heights: Strategic Lessons from Complex Operations,* ed. Michael Miklaucic, Center for Complex Operations and the Center for Technology and National Security Policy (July 2009): 4.

[4] Dan Green, "Counterinsurgency Diplomacy: Political Advisors at the Operational and Tactical Levels," *Military Review* (June 2008): 108.

[5] Ibid.,109

[6] United States Dept of the Army, *The U.S. Army/Marine Corps Counterinsurgency Field Manual:* U.S. Field Manual 3-24: Marine Corps Warfighting Publication no. 3-33.5 (Chicago, The University of Chicago Press, 2007),171.

[7] U.S. Department of the Army, *The Army Universal Task List,* Field Manual 7-15, (Washington, DC: U.S. Department of the Army, February 2009), 7-19.

[8] Chairmen of the Joint Chiefs of Staff, *Joint Operations,* Joint Publication 3-0, (Washington DC: U.S.Joint Chiefs of Staff) A-4.

[9] FORSCOM Message: *Predeployment Training Guidance for Follow-On Forces Deploying ISO Southwest Asia OIF/OEF,* 19 November 2009, https://1anet.first.army.mil/ commandertrainingtool/Download_Document.aspx?index=950 (accessed January 10, 2010).

[10] David C. Gompert and John Gordon IV, *Countering Insurgency in the Muslim World: Rethinking U.S. Priorities and Capabilities,* linked from RAND Counterinsurgency Study – Final Report, 2008, http://www.rand.org/pubs/research_briefs/RB9326/index1.html p: 3 (accessed January 10, 2010.).

[11] John A. Nagl, "A Better War in Afghanistan," Joint Forces Quarterly, issue 56, (1st Quarter 2010): 38.

[12] United States Dept of the Army, *The U.S. Army/Marine Corps Counterinsurgency Field*, 171.

[13] Green, *Counterinsurgency Diplomacy*, 108.

[14] Dexter Filkins, "His Long War," *New York Times Magazine,* October 18, 2009: 45.

[15] Nagl, "A Better War in Afghanistan,": 38.

[16] Michael Phillips, "In Afghanistan, Getting to Know the Neighbors is Half the Battle," The Wall Street Journal, July 18, 2008.

[17] *Republic of Iraq District Government Field Manual,* Center for Army Lessons Learned (CALL), (May, 07 2008):4.

[18] Ibid., 4-13.

[19] *The Army Universal Task* List, Field Manual 7-15, 7-19.

[20] The U.S. Army/Marine Corps Counterinsurgency Field Manual, 71.

[21] Herring and Rangwala, *Iraq in Fragments*, 49.

[22] Ibid., 24.

[23] Ibid., 88, 89.

[24] Ibid., 45.

[25] *Republic of Iraq District Government Field Manual,* Center for Army Lessons Learned, 9.

[26] Ibid., 6.

[27] bid., 17.

[28] Thomas Freidman, "Not Good Enough," New York Times, October 14, 2009, 1.

[29] Nagl, "A Better War in Afghanistan," 38.

[30] Herring and Rangwala, *Iraq in Fragments*, 263.

[31] The U.S. Army/Marine Corps Counterinsurgency Field Manual, 179.

[32] David Galula, *Counterinsurgency Warfare: Theory and Practice* (Westport, CT: Praeger Security International, 1964, 2006), 90.

[33] Herring and Rangwala, *Iraq in Fragments*, 78.

[34] Ibid., 68.

[35] Ibid., 60.

[36] Michael M. Philips, "In Afghanistan, Getting to Know the Neighbors is Half the Battle," *Wall Street Journal*, July 18, 2008, 2.

[37] Ibid.

[38] The U.S. Army/Marine Corps Counterinsurgency Field Manual, excerpt by President John F. Kennedy,77.

[39] *A Foreign Affairs Budget for the Future: Fixing the Crisis in Diplomatic Readiness*, American Academy of Diplomacy, (October 2008), http://www.academyofdiplomacy.org/ publications (accessed 10 November 2009).

[40] Office of the Special Representative for Afghanistan and Pakistan, *Afghanistan and Pakistan Regional Stabilization Strategy*, January 2010 (Washington DC, Department of State), 3.

[41] Bay Fang, "A 'Reluctant Warrior' in Iraq," U.S. News & World Report, January 9, 2006, 18.

[42] Galula, *Counterinsurgency Warfare: Theory and Practice*, p5.

[43] Ibid.,p54.

[44] Gompert and Gordon, *Countering Insurgency in the Muslim World: Rethinking U.S. Priorities and Capabilities*, 2.

[45] The U.S. Army/Marine Corps Counterinsurgency Field Manual, 72.

[46] Barno, "Command in Afghanistan 2003-2005: Three Key Lessons Learned" in *Commanding Heights: Strategic Lessons from Complex Operations*,1.

[47] Ibid.,1

[48] Ibid.,4

[49] Ibid., 2.

[50] Ibid., 2.

[51] The U.S. Army/Marine Corps Counterinsurgency Field Manual, 84.

[52] Galula, *Counterinsurgency Warfare: Theory and Practice*, 91.

[53] Ibid., 90.

[54] MG Michael Flynn, "Fixing Intel: A Blueprint for Making Intelligence Relevant in Afghanistan," Center for a New American Security (January 2010): 4.

[55] Ibid.

[56] Phillips, "In Afghanistan, Getting to Know the Neighbors is Half the Battle,"

[57] Ibid.

[58] U.S Department of the Army, *Operational Adaptability: Operating under Conditions of Uncertainty and Complexity in an Era of Persistent Conflict*, TRADOC Pam 525-3-0, (Fort Monroe, VA: Training and Doctrine Command, December 21, 2009),11-12.

[59] Gian P. Gentile, "The Imperative for an American General Purpose Army That Can Fight," *Foreign Policy Research Institute,* (Summer 2009), 460.

[60] Ibid., 457.

[61] Flynn, "Fixing Intel: A Blueprint for Making Intelligence Relevant in Afghanistan,"15

[62] Major Frank D. Pelli, *Insurgency, Counterinsurgency, and the Marines in Vietnam* (Quantico, VA: Combined Staff College, 1990), 13.

[63] The U.S. Army/Marine Corps Counterinsurgency Field Manual, 74.

[64] Pelli, *Insurgency, Counterinsurgency, and the Marines in Vietnam,*14.

[65] The U.S. Army/Marine Corps Counterinsurgency Field Manual, 74.

[66] Christopher D. Kolenda, *Winning Afghanistan at the Community Level*, Joint Forces Quarterly,no. 56 (1st Quarter, 2010), 31.

[67] Ibid.

[68] T.E. Lawrence, *The Evolution of A Revolt*, Army Quarterly and Defense Journal, October 1920, (Devon, United Kingdom). Accessed on 12 Mar 2010 through Command and General Staff College reprint: http://www.cgsc.edu/carl/resources/csi/lawrence/lawrence.asp.